3/26/2019

D1518809

CRAYFISH

by Meg Gaertner

Cody Koala
An Imprint of Pop!
popbooksonline.com

abdobooks.com

Published by Pop!, a division of ABDO, PO Box 398166, Minneapolis, Minnesota 55439. Copyright © 2019 by POP, LLC. International copyrights reserved in all countries. No part of this book may be reproduced in any form without written permission from the publisher. Pop!™ is a trademark and logo of POP, LLC.

Printed in the United States of America, North Mankato, Minnesota

092018
012019

THIS BOOK CONTAINS
RECYCLED MATERIALS

Cover Photo: Shutterstock Images
Interior Photos: Shutterstock Images, 1, 5 (top), 11, 14, 19; iStockphoto, 5 (bottom left), 5 (bottom right), 6–7, 8, 13; Suzanne Long/Alamy, 17; Gary Meszaros/Science Source, 20

Editor: Charly Haley
Series Designer: Laura Mitchell

Library of Congress Control Number: 2018950114

Publisher's Cataloging-in-Publication Data

Names: Gaertner, Meg, author.
Title: Crayfish / by Meg Gaertner.
Description: Minneapolis, Minnesota: Pop!, 2019 | Series: Pond animals | Includes online resources and index.
Identifiers: ISBN 9781532162060 (lib. bdg.) | ISBN 9781641855778 (pbk) | ISBN 9781532163128 (ebook)
Subjects: LCSH: Crayfish--Juvenile literature. | Crawdads--Juvenile literature. | Pond animals--Juvenile literature. | Crustaceans--Juvenile literature.
Classification: DDC 595.384--dc23

Hello! My name is

Cody Koala

Pop open this book and you'll find QR codes like this one, loaded with information, so you can learn even more!

Scan this code* and others like it while you read, or visit the website below to make this book pop.

popbooksonline.com/crayfish

*Scanning QR codes requires a web-enabled smart device with a QR code reader app and a camera.

Table of Contents

Chapter 1

Pond Lobster

Crayfish are **crustaceans**. They look like little lobsters. They can be yellow, red, brown, or green.

Watch a video here!

A crayfish's

head ends in a sharp **snout**.

Its eyes are on short moving stems. A crayfish also has a tail.

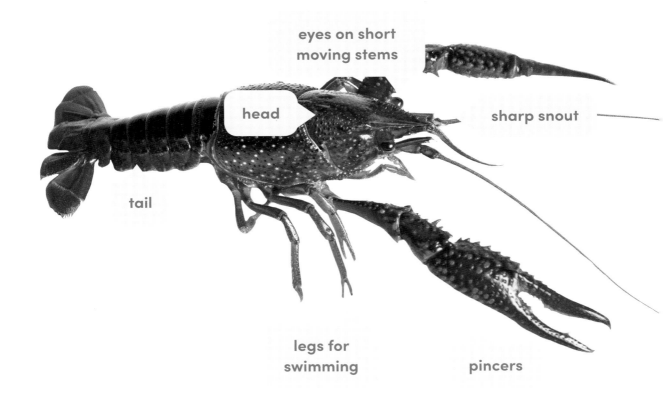

eyes on short
moving stems

sharp snout

head

tail

legs for
swimming

pincers

Crayfish have five pairs of legs. The front pair ends in strong **pincers**. The four back pairs are smaller. They are used for swimming.

Most crayfish grow to be 3 inches long.

Fresh Water

Crayfish mostly live in streams and lakes. There are about 600 types of crayfish. Most live in North America.

Learn more here!

Food and Protection

Crayfish hide under logs or rocks during the day. They come out at night. They eat worms, plants, snails, young insects and frogs, and more.

Learn more here!

Crayfish mostly move slowly. But they can use their strong tails to move quickly away from danger. They can defend themselves with their pincers.

Crayfish also use their pincers to cut up food.

Crayfish have a hard **exoskeleton** for protection. They shed the exoskeleton and grow a new one. This is how they grow bigger.

Chapter 4

The Life of a Crayfish

Female crayfish lay eggs in the spring. The eggs stay attached to her for five to eight weeks. The eggs hatch, and baby crayfish are born.

Complete an activity here!

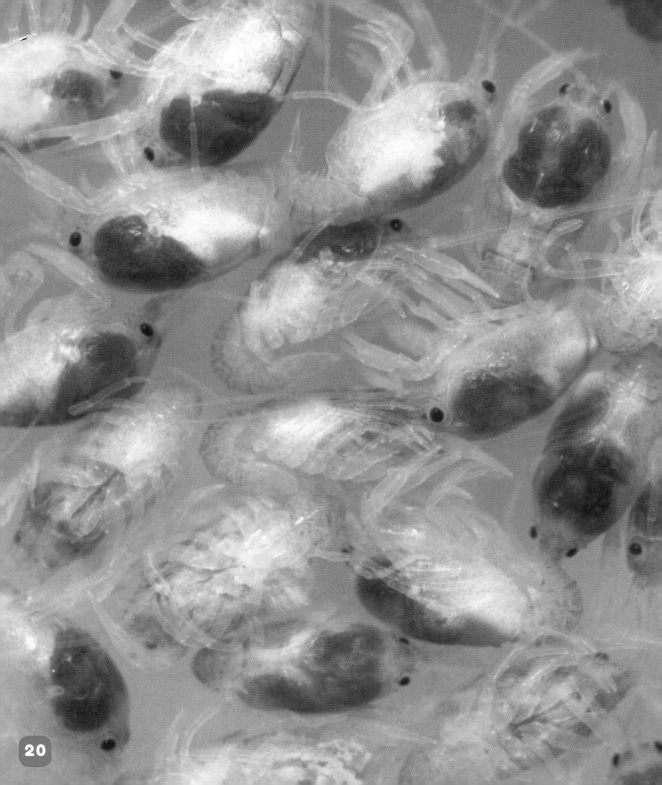

The baby crayfish stay attached to their mother for several weeks. They shed their exoskeletons three times. Then they are big enough to live on their own.

Different types of crayfish can live between one and 20 years.

Making Connections

Text-to-Self

Have you ever seen a crayfish? If not, have you seen another animal in the wild?

Text-to-Text

Have you read another book about a different animal? How is that animal similar to a crayfish? How is it different?

Text-to-World

Scientists put crayfish and similar animals into a group called crustaceans. What other animals are similar to each other but not the same?

Glossary

crustacean – a member of a group of animals with exoskeletons that live in water, such as crabs, lobsters, crayfish, or shrimp.

exoskeleton – a hard covering that protects and supports the body for some types of animals.

female – a person or animal of the sex that can have babies or lay eggs.

pincer – the front claw of a crustacean.

snout – the nose of an animal.

Index

Online Resources

popbooksonline.com

Thanks for reading this Cody Koala book!

Scan this code* and others like it in this book, or visit the website below to make this book pop!

popbooksonline.com/crayfish

*Scanning QR codes requires a web-enabled smart device with a QR code reader app and a camera.